I0164530

What the Scripture says about Homosexuality

A Biblical Look At Homosexuality - Lesbianism

Gilbert James

Into Thine Hand
Publishing with a biblical perspective
4141 NW 39th Ave
Fort Lauderdale, FL 33309
www.intothinehand.com

The Unnatural Family Structure
A Biblical Look At Homosexuality - Lesbianism

Published by
Into Thine Hand
4141 NW 39th Ave
Fort Lauderdale FL 33309
www.intothinehand.com

ISBN: 978-0-9841231-5-5

The Unnatural Family Structure

A Biblical Look At Homosexuality - Lesbianism

Table of Contents

Who Wrote the
Manual on Homosexuality?

You ask how early in human existence has the issue of homosexuality and homosexuals been identified in societies of the past? Is homosexuality and homosexuals just a now phenomenon? The issue of homosexuality has been sited way back in the beginning book of the biblical history of humanity, Geneses as well as the latter books of the New Testament.

You ask how have societies of the past handled both the persons involved in the act of homosexuality and the act itself? While within the clan of the homosexuals, the perspective on their treatment may understandably be favorable in nature, how have the societies outside of their clan perceived and treated them and their lifestyle?

Most of all, you ask, how has the Divine Creator of humanity handled both the homosexuals and homosexuality? Is He even a factor in this matter and if so, does He even have the right to be? Doesn't He, that is the Creator of humanity need an invitation from humanity to legitimatize His involvement in our society or daily matters, including the homosexuals and their lifestyle?

The unnatural family structure

Does the designer of the watch have the right to accompany that watch with a manual or has the watch, just by being in existence gained the right to determine its operational dogmas baring its designer? Does the maker of your vehicle that you may have owned or now own have the right to accompany that vehicle with its manual or does the vehicle have the right to determine its own operational dogmas?

In truth and in fact, the Scriptures which is the manual that the Creator of humanity has sent out with same, have a wealth of dogmas regarding the operations of humanity. This includes those who engage in the act of homosexuality and the act itself.

I trust that you will incline yourself to the uncovering of the overwhelming amount of references in the Creator's manual, that He has sent with humanity whom He has created, regarding both the homosexuals and homosexuality. Contrary to the belief that the Creator of humanity has been silent or mum on the issue of the homosexuals and their lifestyle, He has been very loud in His Word. Contrary to the belief that His Word has said very little or nothing on this issue, He has spoken volumes. As such, let's let *"the Word"* speak.

Chapter 1
How Does the Scripture Classify HomosexualityLesbianism ?

The subject of homosexuality lesbianism and beastiology are placed into the same category of offence, rather, sin under the biblical classification of moral deviation. The biblical definition of homosexuality and lesbianism is the male or female gender lying with or engaging in sexual relations with its own gender as with the opposite gender.

Beastology is classified in the Bible as mankind (male or fe male) lying with or engaging in sexual relations with the beast or animal as they would do with humankind. Though beastiology appears to be of a more deteriorated human engagement, the Bible deemed such act as being on the same level with homosexualitand lesbianism .

The following scripture passage speaks to these classifications. Leviticus eighteen verses twenty-two through twenty-three says: *22. Thou shalt not lie with mankind, as with womankind it is abomination 23. Neither shalt thou lie with any beast to defile thyself therewith: neither shall any woman stand before a beast to lie down thereto: it is confusion.*

9

What the Scripture says about Homosexuality

The word abomination used in verse twenty-two of Leviticus eighteen means a disgusting thing, wickedness or defiance per Strongs Number Reference.

The term *disgusting* points to the recipient of the offence (who is God in this instance) as being fed-up with the act and deems it as outrageously intolerable.

Wickedness as used in this context refers to a conscious and deliberate effort to provoke the recipient of the offence. A proper illustration of this would be like your neighbor knowing that you despised the idea of filth on your lawn and make it their duty to store their filth and pour it on your lawn, like not only once, but like every day or every week.

The term *Defiance* refers to a conscious and deliberate effort to defy the rules or the law. A proper illustration of this would be like a person knowing that rape is not only a violation against humanity, but also a violation of the law and deliberately went in front of the police station and performed the act of raping a woman right in front of the police.

The Creator of humanity states in His Word that there is no human being on the face of the earth who does not know that this act is a deviation from the way that He, that is God, made them. Let us examine Romans two verses fourteen through fifteen. It says: *14. For when the Gentiles, which have not the law, do by nature the things contained in the law, these, having not the law, are a law unto themselves 15. Which shew the work of the law written in their hearts their conscience also bearing witness, and their thoughts the mean while accusing or else excusing one another;*

Let us examine some key points in the previous passage:
- *"The Gentiles which having no law"* refers to the fact that they had not the literary written law.
- *"A law unto themselves"* speaks to the fact that each person is endowed with their own conscience which is the

human alarm clock.

- *"Do by nature the things contained in the law"* speaks not of all but those who chose to comply with their conscience which alarms them that they were going off course.
- *"The law written in their hearts"* is how the Creator made us. The fact that humanity elects to go in the wrong direction is not due to the absence of the knowledge that wrong is wrong, but rather the conscious choice to do otherwise.
- *"Their thoughts accusing and excusing"* Yes, while their conscience sounds the alarm, their thought process (the mind) determines their conscious direction of choice.

The Creator of humanity, in His Word, takes this deliberate choice of mankind as deviation from that which is right when they knew that their choice was that which was wrong. The creator took it even a bit further. He charged them with not only making a conscious choice to deviate from that which is wrong, but taking pleasure doing so plus conjure up a clan of like practice. Let us examine His words in the book of Romans chapter one verse thirty-two: *Who knowing the judgment of God, that they which commit such things are worthy of death, not only do the same, but have pleasure in them that do them.*

Notice that the Creator of mankind asserted that he, that is *mankind, not only knows when wrong is wrong but he is also aware of the pending judgment from God* his Creator for such acts. It is with that knowledge that he makes the choice to deviate from that which he knows to be right.

Notice further that he, that is *mankind, also elects to affirm, that is to embrace and collaborate with the clan of those who deviate from the moral compass* It is as if he both joins the coop and participates in or embraces the proliferation of such practice or lifestyle.

The author does not believe that there is one person who has assumed the homosexual lifestyle who is not conscious of the fact that at least society is against them. Most, if not all of them are fully aware that there is a moral law against their lifestyle and that the Christian community is against it. Most, of all, they are aware that their Creator is against them, though they may even try to use His very words to justify their deeds or lifestyle.

Because of this abominable lifestyle of the cities of Sodom and Gomorrah the term *sodomy* or *sodomite* was coined. Examine Deuteronomy chapter twenty-three verse seventeen. It says: *There shall be no whore of the daughters of Israel, nor a Sodomite of the sons of Israel.* Also, examine first Kings fourteen verse twenty-four which says *"And there were also sodomites in the land: and they did according to all the abominations of the nations which the LORD cast out before the children of Israel."*

The term *sodomy* or *sodomite* is the label ascribed to the practice and people who made up the population of Sodom and Gomorrah when the angels of God went down and examined it and found that it was in fact existing in the state that God saw from heaven.

The nineteenth chapter of the book of Geneses, verses five and six lets us in on the nature of the practices of the men of Sodom. The passage consists of the actions of the men of Sodom towards the angels of the Lord which the Scripture termed as the men which came in to dwell with Lot's family. Observe: *4 But before they lay down, the men of the city, even the men of Sodom compassed the house round, both old and young, all the people from every quarter: 5 And they called unto Lot, and said unto him, Where are the men which came in to thee this night? bring them out unto us, that we may know them.*

Note that the *'men' of the city, even the "men" of Sodom both young and old,* surrounded Lot's house. Note further that *"all the people from every quarter* were present, *sanctioning* and as such, *having pleasure in* the campaign to solicit the moral deviation of their lifestyle.

Notice further that it was specifically *"the men*öf Sodom who wanted to know *"the men"* who came to visit Lot. So that there is no ambiguity, the term *"to know them"* meant to get in bed with them or to put it bluntly, to have sexual relations with them.

We get a little more insight into the nature of the offence or sin of Sodom and Gomorrah by examining Jude one verses six through seven. It says: *6. And the angels which kept not their first estate, but left their own habitation, he hath reserved in everlasting chains under darkness unto the judgment of the great day. 7. Even as Sodom and Gomorraḥ and the cities about them in like manner, giving themselves over to fornication, and going after strange flesḥ are set forth for an example, suffering the vengeance of eternal fire.*

Let us notice first that their pursuits were highly ambitious in nature in that *they were extremely influential even in reaching the regions beyond their borders* The lifestyle of the home sexuals today assumes the same ambitious pursuits. They seek to influence way beyond their borders, even to the entire world. It is not just we want to be able to do this domestically. It is the ambition of the homosexual clan to proselyte the entire world and bring them into compliance with their perverted perspectives on the family structure.

Notice further that they, that is the people of Sodom and Gomorraḥ *gave themselves over to fornication* Based upon the context present here, the term fornication isn't used in the specific sense where it is about two unmarried people engaging in sexual relations. It refers to a free for all boundary-less free dom to engage in whatever sexual desires pleases the exe cuter of the act. It is a society that embraces a culture that lends itself to a lifestyle of zero accountability to their Creator or even the powers that be within their own society.

As we continue our examination of the passage at hand, we see also that the people of Sodom and Gomorrah carried a lifestyle that was *gone after or pursued strange flesh*. Barnes Notes on the NT explains this reference as follows: The reference seems to be to the peculiar sin which, from the name Sodom, has been called sodomy Comp. Romans 1:27. The meaning of the phrase going after is, that they were greatly addicted to this vice. The word strange, or other, refers to that which is contrary to nature.

The moral state of the cities of Sodoand Gomorrah   was so bad that God could not find ten righteous persons in it.

"When the two angels came to Sodom to warn Lot of the impending doom, they found him sitting in the city gate (Geneses nineteen verse one). This indicates that Sodom was fortified. Bab edh-Dhra, which means 'gate of the arm,' had imposing fortifications. Evidence for settlement was found outside the walls as well. The total population at the time Bab edh-Dhra met its end was between 600 and 1,200."
http://www.biblearchaeology.org/post/2008/04/T he-Discovery-of-the-Sin-Cities-of-Sodom-and-Gomorrahaspx

Thus, God, their Creator had to set an example of them. They suffered "the vengeance of eternal life the passage said. This means that they suffered the loss of eternal life. The ultimate calculation means that they lost heaven and all of their lifetime investments added up to zero dividends in the economy of God, their Creator and in eternity.

They call themselves gay society calls them homosexuals the Bible calls sodomites and their lifestyle sodomy and abomina tion The term "homo" means Disparaging and Offensive... that's what society labeled them as. The term "gay" represents merriness and an upbeat spirit... that's what they choose to call themselves.

Chapter 2
What Does the Scripture Prescribe as the Consequence for Homosexuality - Lesbianism

E xamine what the book of Leviticus chapter twenty and verse thirteen says shall be the fate of the persons who engage in the act of sodomy homosexuality or lesbian ism *If a man also lie with mankind, as he lieth with a woman, both of them have committed an abomination they shall surely be put to death; their blood shall be upon them.*

Note the premise upon which the consequence rests. It is the act of lying or engaging in sexual relations with the same sex the man lying with his own kind, that is his own gender.

Notice also the classification ascribed to this act. It is an abom ination As we recall, an abomination is a disgusting thing, wickedness or defiance It is an openly conscious, in your face provocation which serves as a defiance to the known stan dards or rules.

Finally, lets notice the prescribed consequence They shall be put to death. That punishment which is prescribed by the Scriptures is the death penalty

What the Scripture says about Homosexuality

It took the intervention of the angels to slow down the moral intent of the men of Sodom as outlined in Geneses nineteen verses ten through eleven. It says: *10. But the men put forth their hand, and pulled Lot into the house to them, and shut to the door. 11. And they smote the men that were at the door of the house with blindness, both small and great: so that they wearied themselves to find the door.*

In Genesis nineteen verses twenty-four through twenty-five God destroyed the people of Sodo and Gomorrah and their cities for their indulgence in this lifestyle. Observe: *24 Then the Lord rained upon Sodo and upon Gomorrah brimstone and fire from the Lord out of heaven; 25 And he overthrew those cities, and all the plain, and all the inhabitants of the cities, and that which grew upon the ground.*

"Brimstone and fire" does that seem like an approval or in the least bit an embracing of this lifestyle by God, the Creator? "He, that is God, rained" fire and brimstones upon the cities of Sodom and Gomorrah and their inhabitants. The process of rain represents at least enough to cover all the surface of that terrain. The process of rain could also represent an abundance of supply to flood the surface of that terrain.

Observe that He, that is God, rained fire In actuality, He set the place on fire. A rain of fire signifies that none was intended to survive or escape. The truth is that the Creator burned up the entire twin cities of Sodom and Gomorrah with all of its inhabitants.

That He rained brimstones means that God dropped bombs on that whole area to literally crush both the infrastructure and inhabitants to ruins.

"Brimstone, or sulphur, is found in considerable quantities on the shores of the Dead Sea. (Genesis nineteen verse twenty-four) It is a well-known simple mineral substance, crystalline,

The unnatural family structure

easily melted, very inflammable, and when burning emits a peculiar suffocating odor. It is found in great abundance near volcanoes. The soil around Sodoand Gomorrah abounded in sulphur and bitumen." – Smith's Bible Dictionary –

It is clear again that God, the Creator, not only intended for nothing to survive but no one as well. God doubled up on the magnitude of punishment that He deemed that the people who engage in the homosexual lifestyle deserved. While He was raining fire on Sodom and Gomorrah He was raining brim - stones also.

As to the extent of the damage to Sodoand Gomorrah , the passage said that He, that is God, overthrew the cities of Sodoand Gomorrah . He also included the plains or all the surrounding territories involved.

The passage went on to say that He, that is God, included all the inhabitants of the cities, and that which grew upon the ground. This means that the scope of the affected was massive or all inclusive. As such, we must calculate people, structures, animals, plants that grew upon the ground and the list goes on until all was exhausted. None, yea nothing was left, not even one.

Based upon the writer of the book of Jude verse seven, Sodom and Gomorrah suffered the vengeance of eternal fire meaning that they lost it.

The scripture presents King Asa as having done right when he removed the Sodomites from the land in his rule. Observe what first kings fifteen verses eleven through twelve says: *11. And Asa did that which was right in the eyes of the Lord, as did David his father. 12. And he took away the Sodomites out of the land, and removed all the idols that his fathers had made.*

What the Scripture says about Homosexuality

Let us give credit where credit is due. This passage shows that God the Creator classified what king Asa did, in removing the Sodomites from the land, as being right in His sight (deserving a high five). This affirms the fact that God embraces the absence of the homosexual lifestyle from His economy. The passage also affirms that the structure of both the society and the church that God perceives as right in His sight is one that does not include either the homosexuals or their lifestyle.

Chapter 3
Is This Only a Prohibition in the Levitical laws or Old Testament Pages, which Some Argue Is Not for New Testament Believers and Times?

God has not only shown his disdain for this act in the Old Testament but in the New Testament as well. In the book of Romans, God gave up a generation and turned them over to a reprobate mind for engaging in such acts. Observe what Romans chapter one verses twenty-four through twenty-eight says: *24. Wherefore God also gave them up to uncleanness through the lusts of their own hearts, to dishonour their own bodies between themselves: 25. Who changed the truth of God into a lie, and worshipped and served the creature more than the Creator, who is blessed for ever. Amen. 26. For this cause God gave them up unto vile affections: for even their women did change the natural use into that which is against nature 27. And likewise also the men, leaving the natural use of the woman, burned in their lust one toward another; men with men working that which is unseemly, and receiving in themselves that recompence of their error which was meet (fit). 28. And even as they did not like to retain God in their knowledge God gave them over to a reprobate mind, to do those things which are not convenient;*

"God gave them up" in verse twenty-four through or because of the lusts of their own hearts. It appeared that the lusts of

19

their hearts superseded or even replaced all manner of accountability This included accountability to society and most of all to God, their Creator. That was all that mattered... that is the desires of their hearts. Whatever their desires craved for, that they pursued without regards for any accountability to their society or their Creator. That was the human condition that got God to give them up or write them off, so to speak.

"God gave them up in verse twenty-six through twenty-seven unto vile affections because "26. ...their women did change the natural use into that which is against nature : 27. And likewise also the men, leaving the natural use of the woman, burned in their lust one toward another; men with men working that which is unseemly."

Their women did change the "natural use into that which is "against nature" What this indictment established first of all is that there is indeed a natural, inborn or appropriate use of one's sexual desires and there is an unnatural use of same. It is a natural desire to desire or be attracted to the opposite sex. That is not something that either a young person or an adult should scold themselves for when this occurs. What is potentially explosive or appropriate is what one does with that desire or where one directs or channels same.

Inferencing from the factor of that which is "against nature so-lidifies the fact that the desire of the human being towards the opposite sex is in harmony with the nature of man as his Creator made him. On the contrary, the desire of the human being towards the same sex is both unnatural and against the na - ture of man as his Creator made him.

We are not left to guess what were the dominant desires of their hearts or where their hearts were because the passage amplified it for us. The passage explained that their women did change the natural use into that which is against nature This means that they burned with desires for their own sex.

likewise, also the men, leaving the natural use of the woman, burned in their lust one toward another; men with men working that which is unseemly. As such, the men also left the natural use of the women and channel or directed their desires to wards the same sex.

In many instances, if not most, beauty or the lack thereof; attractiveness or the lack thereof on the part of both the male or the female desiring their own sex is not a factor. It isn't be cause they had no beauty or did not possess any form of attractiveness that would attract their opposite sex. Rather, in many instances, it is quite the opposite. It stemmed from a pre-desire or just a conscious choice to veer across the boundary that the Creator has set.

"God gave them up in verse twenty-eight because they did not like to retain God in their knowledge To live your life with out acknowledging your Creator in all your dealings is to deny your accountability to Him. To live your life from the perspective that you are the god of your life is to deny the fact that you are made by a Creator and He does matter.

This approach won't cut it with God because he is a jealous God, the scripture said. And He has every right to assume that posture because He made you and me for His own pleasure. This fat is seen in Colossians one verse sixteen. Here is what the passage says: For by him were all things created, that are in heaven, and that are in earth, visible and invisible, whether they be thrones, or dominions, or principalities, or powers: all things were created by him, and for him. [Revelation 4:11] *Thou art worthy, O Lord, to receive glory and honour and power: for thou hast created all things, and for thy pleasure they are and were created.*

The New Testament writings not only reflect God giving them up (that is those who assume the homosexual lifestyle) but they (that is the scriptures) also identify them as having no inheritance in the kingdom of God. Since homosexuality is classified as a sin by the scriptures, it, along with any other sin pose as a never for God to endorse. Thus, the scripture represents not only an instance of prohibition, which would be more than enough, but rather a collection of prohibitions throughout the New Testament as well as the Old Testament.

The apostle Paul writes in the book of first Corinthians chapter *six verses nine through eleven the following: 9. Know ye not that the unrighteous shall not inherit the kingdom of God? Be not deceived: neither fornicators, nor idolaters, nor adulterers, nor effeminate nor abusers of themselves with mankind, 10. Nor thieves, nor covetous, nor drunkards, nor revilers, nor extortioners, shall inherit the kingdom of God. 11. And such were some of you: but ye are washed, but ye are sanctified, but ye are justified in the name of the Lord Jesus, and by the Spirit of our God.*

The word effeminate as used in this passage is the Greek word malakovß Malakos (mal-ak-os') which means soft, soft to the touch according to Strongs Number Reference. The same source continues to say that the word was used in reference to a boy kept for homosexual relations with a man, a male who submits his body to unnatural lewdness, a male prostitute.

This word appeared in the book of Matthew chapter eleven verse eight where it says: *But what went ye out for to see? A man clothed in soft raiment? behold, they that wear soft clothing are in kings' houses.* It also appeared in the book of Luke chapter seven verse twenty-five where it says *"But what went ye out for to see? A man clothed in soft raiment? Behold, they which are gorgeously apparelled, and live delicately, are in kings' courts."*

In both passages it is applied to clothing, and translated "soft or gorgeous raiment" which refers to the light, thin garments worn by the rich and great."

However, in first Corinthians it applies to morals. There it denotes those who give themselves up to a soft, luxurious way of living; who make self-indulgence the grand object of life; who can endure no hardship, and practice no self-denial in the cause of duty and of God. – Barnes Notes on the New Testament --

The technical word for "a boy used in pederasty "sexual relations between two males, especially when one of them is a minor... a boy or youth who is in a sexual relationship with a man. Those who suffered this abuse were likewise called pathics. -- Coffman NT Commentary –

Abusers of themselves with men were the sodomites. Regarding the passive and active homosexuals referred to in these words, it should be remembered that an apostle of Jesus Christ condemned such persons in the judgment that they shall not inherit the kingdom of God. What is to be thought of churches which not only condone this sin, but in widely publicized cases have actually ordained homosexuals to the ministry? It is the judgment of this writer that churches exhibiting such a total disregard of the New Testament have, in so doing, forfeited all identity with Christianity -- Coffman NT Commentary –

God under the writings of the apostle Paul not only labeled the act of the Sodomic lifestyle as unrighteous but the ones who carry such lifestyle... that is the person who is doing the act.

There is no reference in this passage that supports the claim by practicing Sodomites that this is a genetically born trait that cannot be cured or reversed. In fact, there is a reference in the passage which contradicts such claim.

What the Scripture says about Homosexuality

Verse eleven of first Corinthians chapter six brings that out. Observe: And such 'were' some of you but ye are washed, but ye are sanctified, but ye are justified in the name of the Lord Jesus, and by the Spirit of our God.

Chapter 4
Who Is the Author of the Family Structure and who Has the Residual Rights to Determine and Distribute the Correct Family Structure?

B e it known that the author of the family is God and He alone owns the copyrights to the family structure. Thus, the entity that endeavors to pull from or continue to draw from the pages of His manual for His creation correctly has the residual rights to determine and distribute the correct structure for the family.

The world should not be instructing the church or serve to influence her regarding the correct structure of the family… it should be the other way around where the church should be instructing the world and serve to influence it regarding the correct structure of the family. If the New Testament church (which she should) which holds the Bible as her final authority. As such, she alone has the residual rights to determine and distribute to all other entities what the correct structure of the family should be.

Concerning the original structure of the family as the mold was established by its designer who is God, the book of Geneses chapter two verses twenty-one through twenty-five is clear as to who the author or designer of the family was and how it should be structured. God set up a family of husband and wife male and female, married, and instituted the proliferation of the human race from that structure. Observe: *21 And the Lord God caused a deep sleep to fall upon Adam, and he slept: and he took one of his ribs, and closed up the flesh instead thereof; 22 And the rib which the Lord God had taken from man, made he a woman, and brought her unto the man. 23 And Adam said, This is now bone of my bones, and flesh of my flesh: she shall be called Woman, because she was taken out of Man 24 Therefore shall a man leave his father and his mother, and shall cleave unto his wife and they shall be one flesh 25 And they were both naked, the man and his wife and were not ashamed*

Notice that it is the Lord, man's Creator who caused a deep sleep to fall upon Adam. The word 'caused' denotes an actively initiated act by the Lord. This means that it was the Lord who actively put the man to sleep to take the rib from him. It was involuntary on the part of Adam... the Creator conducted the entire process. Here we are presented with the first anesthetic surgery.

The only difference is that when the Lord was finished with His surgery, the body was completely healed immediately as against the surgery that man performs which requires a process of time to heal the body. The scripture says that the Lord took one of his ribs and closed-up the flesh. That constitutes a surgery with no spot or blemish remaining immediately. That is a characteristic that is exclusive to the Creator.

Note further that it was the Lord who used the rib which He had removed from the man and made the woman. The word used for 'woman' in this passage means "out of man" This signifies that the man needs the woman to be complete and the woman needs the man to be complete in a family union. A man and a man and a woman and a woman   in a family union is an incomplete domestic or family union.

It is very important to understand that the words in verses twenty-four through twenty-five of Geneses chapter two were spoken by the Lord instead of Adam. In the first place, note the wording of the statement which is in the third person instead of the first. The personal pronoun "his" instead of "my", "they" instead of "we" is used. Observe also the words of Jesus in Matthew nineteen verses three through six: *4 And he answered and said unto them, Have ye not read, that he which made them at the beginning made them male and female, 5 And said, For this cause shall a man leave father and mother, and shall cleave to his wife: and they twain shall be one flesh? 6 Wherefore they are no more twain, but one flesh. What therefore God hath joined together, let not man put asunder.*

To consider a union between humanity of the same sex a family (other than blood relation) and further, to consider them legitimate married couples, not only is an abomination to God, but an assault upon the true structure of the family setup by the author of the family

The establishment of marriage the structure and development of the family is a theocratic responsibility not political, it is a Christian responsibility and not secular. It is the Christians who should be telling the world how to setup and operate their families, not the world telling the Christians or the world how to setup and operate families. It is clear that Christians are not assuming their roles as the salt of the earth. Christians are not subscribing to the biblical principles of running their families why the divorce rate is the same in the Christian community as it is in the world's.

If God wanted two of the same sex to make up the family structure He would have just made another man. He made the first one, all He had to do was duplicate the process. So it is clear that the instigator, initiator, establisher and owner of the family structure did not intend for it to be made up of two of the same sex. The scripture says that He brought HER to the MAN, not him to the man.

God put it into the man to want a 100% woman.. soft, tender, loving WOMAN! In discussion, a lady said to me a while back: If you as the man hand me the hammer, don't complain when I start massaging you and my hand is rough. It is clear that men have handed the women the hammer a long time ago and gone Gerry-curling.

God put it into the woman to want THE MAN… 100% man! A man strong but still sensitive to her needs based on his knowledge of her. (1st Peter three verse seven) *Likewise, ye husbands, dwell with them according to knowledge, giving honour unto the wife, as unto the weaker vessel, and as being heirs together of the grace of life; that your prayers be not hindered.*

How can you know a woman when you met her tonight and you are in bed with her tonight? Giving her honor as the weaker vessel…. Ladies, I didn't say that the woman is the weaker vessel, the Bible says so, yea, God, her Creator and the originator of the family said so.

Yes, we know that you women can prove to men that you can be the joint chief of staffs and the commanders of the military but your true nature is in the home as primary. Your heart of hearts is in the home. Deep down, you desire to be loved, cared for and cherished You know how I know that? Because God made you so! That's what He said.

The author does not believe that the scripture teaches that the woman is weaker intellectually… In many cases, he believes that they may be even stronger in that area. He believes that the scripture teaches that the woman is weaker emotionally and physically.

The unnatural family structure

The first purpose for the establishment of marriage and the family is companionship. Let us examine Geneses two verse eighteen. Here is what it says: *And the Lord God said, It is not good that the man should be alone; I will make him an help meet (fit) for him.* The same sex cannot be meet or be fit for marital partnership (companionship) in the family structure be cause God made them with missing pieces that can only be complete with a member of the opposite sex. The man needs his rib and the woman needs the man because she came from him. They are interdependent.

There are mental, emotional and physical gaps in both sexes that can only be complete by the opposite sex to constitute a proper marriage and a proper family. The children have needs that can only be fulfilled by a mother and they also have needs that can only be fulfilled by a father.

One of the primary, if not the primary purpose for the estab lishment of the family is procreation.. multiplication of the na tions. Two genders of the same type cannot effectively fulfill that purpose. God repeated His procreation purpose for the family to Noah and his family after the flood as is seen in the book of Geneses eight verses fifteen through seventeen. Ob serve: *15. And God spake unto Noah, saying, 16. Go forth of the ark, thou, and thy wife, and thy sons, and thy sons' wives with thee. 17. Bring forth with thee every living thing that is with thee, of all flesh, both of fowl, and of cattle, and of every creep ing thing that creepeth upon the earth; that they may breed abundantly in the earth, and be fruitful, and multiply upon the earth.*

Marital union is a picture of Christ and the church. The church is always portrayed throughout the scriptures in the feminine gender and as the bride and Christ in the masculine gender, as the Groom, except for minor references to the church in the neuter gender.

Chapter 5
Practical Questions and Answers on the Issue of Homosexuality and Lesbianism

Question: What if someone draws your attention to 2 Cor. 11:2 *"For I am jealous over you with godly jealousy: for I have espoused you to one husband, that I may present you as a chaste virgin to Christ."* The person went on to pose the following inferences:

- The apostle Paul, who was a male expressed his jealousy over a body of both male and female.
- The Bible says here that both male and female are going to marry to Christ who is a male and so we are just living this out until we get to heaven.

Answer:

- This jealousy of the apostle Paul was not a jealousy that's found in the flesh or the physical because he qualified it by saying his jealousy was a godly jealousy
- The Greek word used here for jealous is the word zhlovw Zeloo (dzay-lo'-o) which means zealous or filled with zeal.

Question: Someone says to you, is there a specific scripture reference that directly speaks against homosexual lifestyle?

Answer:

The unnatural family sructure

- [Leviticus 18:22-23] *Thou shalt not lie with mankind, as with womankind it is abomination 23. Neither shalt thou lie with any beast to defilethyself therewith: neither shall any woman stand before a beast to lie down thereto: it is confusion.*
- [Leviticus 20:13] *If a man also lie with mankind, as he lieth with a woman, both of them have committed an abomination: they shall surely be put to death; their blood shall be upon them.*
- [Rom. 1:26-27] 26. *For this cause God gave them up unto vile affections: for even their women did change the natural use into that which is against nature 27. And likewise also the men, leaving the natural use of the woman, burned in their lust one toward another; men with men working that which is unseemly, and receiving in themselves that reompence of their error which was meet.*
- [1 Cor. 6:9] *Know ye not that the unrighteoushall not in - herit the kingdom of God? Be not deceived: neither fornicators, nor idolaters, nor adulterers, nor effeminate nor abusers of themselves with mankind,*

Question: Someone brings to your attention [Gal. 3:28] *"There is neither Jew nor Greek, there is neither bond nor free, there is neither male nor female for ye are all one in Christ Jesus."* and says to you, God is not concerned about the distinction of the genders because the Bible says there is neither male nor female

Answer:

- That scripture answers itself with a qualifier: in Christ Jesus… this is strictly addressing the Christian's spiritual position in Christ as far as our salvation is concerned, not in a family setting or everyday earthly life experience.
- In reference to the family setting, God specifically highlights the distinction of the genders.
  - [Gen. 1:27-28] 27. *So God created man in his own image, in the image of God created he him; male and*

female created he them. 28. And God blessed them, and God said unto them, Be fruitful, and multiply and replenish the earth, and subdue it: and have dominion over the fish of the sea, and over the fowl of the air, and over every living thing that moveth upon the earth.

- *[Eph. 5:23] For the husband is the head of the wife, even as Christ is the head of the church: and he is the saviour of the body.*

Question: Someone says to you this Is a born trait that I did not contribute to and therefore, I cannot change.

Answer:

- If this were a born trait, why did the Bible refer to *such prac tice as unnatural affection and a dishonor?* [Romans 1:24-27] *24. Wherefore God also gave them up to uncleanness through the lusts of their own hearts, to dishonour their own bodies between themselves: 25. Who changed the truth of God into a lie, and worshipped and served the creature more than the Creator, who is blessed for ever. Amen. 26. For this cause God gave them up unto vile affections: for even their women did change the natural use into that which is against nature 27. And likewise also the men, leaving the natural use of the woman, burned in their lust one toward another; men with men working that which is unseemly, and receiving in themselves that recompence of their error which was meet.*

- If this were a born trait, *why did the scripture labels those who engage in such acts as unrighteous?* [1 Cor. 6:9] *Know ye not that the unrighteous shall not inherit the kingdom of God? Be not deceived: neither fornicators, nor idolaters, nor adulterers, nor effeminate, nor abusers of themselves with mankind,*

- If this were a born trait that cannot be changed or reversed why did the scripture say that ***such were some of us*** who are now washed, sanctified, and justified in Jesus? (con tinuing from verse nine) [1 Cor. 6:10] *Nor thieves, nor cov* *etous, nor drunkards, nor revilers, nor extortioners, shall inherit the kingdom of God. 11. And **such were some of you** but **ye are washed** but **ye are sanctified** but **ye are justified** in the name of the Lord Jesus, and by the Spirit of our God.*

Question: What are some of the early symptoms to watch out for and what are some life experiences that contribute to this choice of lifestyle?

Answers: Some Early Signs are:

- Children playing with the same sex more than they play with the opposite sex.
- Children Isolating themselves just the two of them, frequently separating from their peer group into isolation.
- Children frequently expressing a desire to assume the roles of the opposite sex as preference.

Note: Not all of these suggestions are original with the author.

Question: What are some life experiences that influence homosexual tendencies?

Answer:

- A female not having a father figure and a male not having a father figure in the home
- Peer pressure and the urge to experiment
- There is a philosophy going around in the public schools, you need to prove to yourself that you are not gay by experimenting with the act.
- There is no need for experimentation because God made the parts to fit.
- Lack of available opposite sex

Question: Are we as Christian going to win the battle against the gay and lesbian community?

Answer: Emphatically No!... because:

What the Scripture says about Homosexuality

- The scripture tells us that the majority will choose a lifestyle of perversion and few will choose life. [Matt. 7:13-14] *13. Enter ye in at the strait gate: for wide is the gate, and broad is the way, that leadeth to destruction, and many there be which go in thereat: 14. Because strait is the gate, and narrow is the way, which leadeth unto life, and few there be that find it.*

- This lifestyle is numbered among end time characteristics [2 Timothy 3:1-3] *1. This know also, that in the last days perilous times shall come. 2. For men shall be lovers of their own selves, covetous, boasters, proud, blasphemers, disobedient to parents, unthankful, unholy, 3. Without natural affection, trucebreakers, false accusers, incontinent, fierce, despisers of those that are good,*

Question: Are we to decrease or stop our opposition and even militancy against that lifestyle?

Answer:

- The answer lies in the scenario of the masses choosing destruction over live and the great commission but 'few' still make a conscious choice to embrace the narrow way. Which one will you and I be associated with? [Matt. 7:13-14] 13. *Enter ye in at the strait gate: for wide is the gate, and broad is the way, that leadeth to destruction, and many there be which go in thereat: 14. Because strait is the gate, and narrow is the way, which leadeth unto life, and few there be that find it.*

- In light of that reality, do we slow down on the great commission or stop going and teaching? [Matt. 28:19-20] *19. Go ye therefore, and teach all nations, baptizing them in the name of the Father, and of the Son, and of the Holy Ghost: 20. Teaching them to observe all things whatsoever I have commanded you: and, lo, I am with you alway, even unto the end of the world. Amen.*

- The same answer goes for our stands against the lifestyle of the homosexuals and lesbians.

Question: Are those who choose the homosexual and lesbian lifestyle written off by God and are doomed for eternity… are they a credible candidate for the gospel?

Answer:

- In Genesis 19 God destroyed the people of Sodom and Gomorrah and their cities for their indulgence for this lifestyle… did God write them off?
- In Gen. 18:-20-21 God Sought for an opportunity to spear them *"20. And the Lord said, Because the cry of Sodom and Gomorrah is great, and because their sin is very grievous; 21. I will go down now, and see whether they have done altogether according to the cry of it, which is come unto me; and if not, I will know."*
- Gen. 18:32 closes the book on God's heart towards the people of Sodoand Gomorrah . "And he said, Oh let not the Lord be angry, and I will speak yet but this once: Peradventure ten shall be found there. And he said, I will not destroy it for ten's sake."
- Now, Did God write them off? The answer is yes and no… Yes because at some point, God had to carry through with His judgment of sin. No because they wrote themselves off by choosing a lifestyle of sin.
- [Romans 1:24] *"Wherefore God also gave them up to uncleanness through the lusts of their own hearts, to dishonour their own bodies between themselves:"* The underlined reason why God gave them up was because of the effects of their own lust.
- [Romans 1:28] *"And even as they did not like to retain God in their knowledge God gave them over to a reprobate mind, to do those things which are not convenient;"* Note that they were the ones who refused to retain their Creator in their knowledge. This drew the Lord into taking the action that was taken.
- Now, Did God write them off?… Yes and No… yes, be cause He had to carry out is judgment of a lifestyle of sin

35

and no because they chose the lifestyle that they were engaged in which required the judgment of God.
- Before we as believers get cocky lets read [1 Cor. 6:9-11]
  9. Know ye not that the unrighteous shall not inherit the kingdom of God? Be not deceived: neither fornicators, nor idolaters, nor adulterers, nor effeminate nor abusers of themselves with mankind, 10. Nor thieves, nor covetous, nor drunkards, nor revilers, nor extortioners, shall inherit the kingdom of God. 11. And such were some of you : but ye are washed, but ye are sanctified, but ye are justified in the name of the Lord Jesus, and by the Spirit of our God.

Questions: What about children of Christians or traditional family members who choose the homosexual lifestyle.. how are you to view and treat them?

Answer:
- We must set the record straight that while we do not and cannot condone the act, we love the person. While they are still our sons and daughters which we are not seeking to reverse, we must establish a mark which serves to main tain respect to the spiritual boundaries within our homes and our biblical convictions.
- A Pentecostal Christian couple have lost their high court claim that they were discriminated against by a local authority because they insisted on their right to tell young foster children that homosexuality is morally wrong. Eunice and Owen Johns, who are in their sixties and have fostered children in the past, claimed they were being discriminated against by Derby city council because of their Christian beliefs, after they told a social worker they could not tell a child a "homosexual lifestyle" was acceptable. www.the guardian.com/society/2011/feb/28/christian-couple-lose-care-case
- We cannot turn a blind eye to the symptoms and charac teristics of girls with girls and boys with boys anymore. It has come to that right where we are at the moment.

Index

such were some of us 32
such were some of you 22, 33, 36

T

ten righteous 14
the moral compass 11
the unrighteous 22 31 32 36
their own sex 20, 21
theocratic responsibility 27
there is neither male nor female 31
they shall be one flesh 26
this Is a born trait 32
thoughts accusing and excusing 11
turned them over to a reprobate mind 19
two of the same sex to make up the family structure 27

U

unnatural affection 32
urge to experiment 33

V

vengeance of eternal life 14

W

weaker emotionally 28
weaker intellectually 28
Wickedness 10 15
womankind: it is abomination. 23. Neither shalt thou lie with
any beast to defile 9, 31
written off 35

Z

Zeloo (dzay-lo'-o) which means zealous 30